AMAZING
PLANTS
OF THE WORLD

Albatros

CHAPTER I.

Hey, you've found it! Welcome to my botanical garden, overgrown after some long rainy years, some hot sunny years, and many, many years without visitors like you. It was once a paradise, a plant paradise, I must say. Plants bloomed as they wished, their stems growing, climbing, and twining all around everything that got in their way, their leaves stretching far and wide, and among all that beauty, there I was. I lived happily, ripening into a plant myself! Who else but me, the botanist Dr. Carnation? Well, since you have already arrived, already invaded my kingdom, come and take a peek at my pride and joy. Are you carrying handkerchiefs and some perfume to cover the stench? If not, fetch them quickly, as you can't do without them in my first pavilion of plant beauties, which, eh, smells quite strange. I am already used to them, but be assured that you won't be able to stand it. Well then, are we ready and steady? Keep your handkerchiefs at your noses and let's go!

DEAD HORSE
ARUM LILY

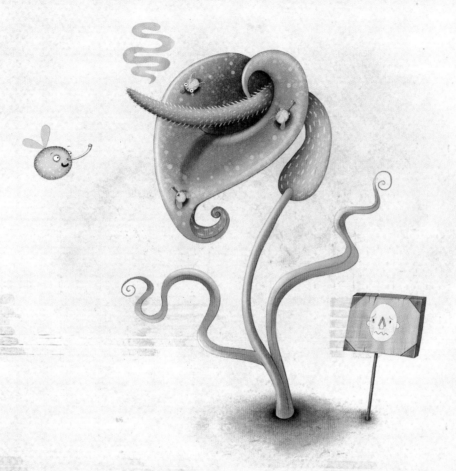

Come on, now. Stop searching for the dead horse. It's not around, neither alive nor dead. Though I well understand how this smell could make you think that just around the corner you might stumble upon a carcass. However, the culprit is this beautiful plant: *helicodiceros muscivorus*. When it blooms, it simply stinks! It can for sure dissuade us delicate people. We might run away in disgust, rather than examine this charming flower.

However, it is exactly the opposite for flies. *Helicodiceros muscivorus* smells so nice to them that they descend upon it in great numbers. And they are not alone! In addition to flies, lots of basking lizards can be found on it! Actually, this plant also radiates heat. Why not make use of this warmth, the lizards think. And, as a bonus, the lizards can stuff their faces with any unobservant flies.

4

JACKAL FOOD

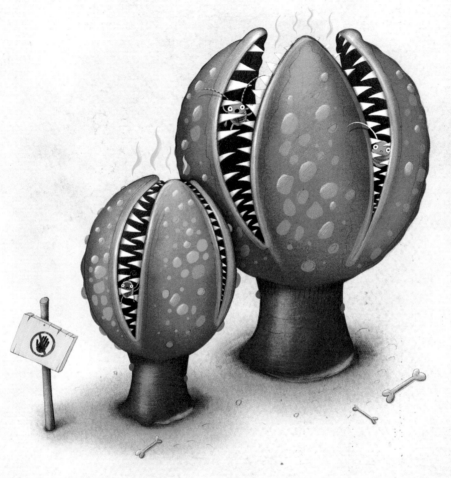

This parasitic plant—my favorite beauty from Africa!—might look like a monster from outer space and smell like rotten meat, but rest assured, it won't hurt you. It has no leaves and hides the buds of its flowers underground, but it's not shy at all! When the time comes, it shoots to the surface and after precious rain it blooms in an attractive orange-red color. *Come check me out*, the flower cries to beetles, luring them with its color, attracting them with its smell. And as soon as it lures them in, it imprisons the intoxicated beetles in the flower chamber. For this reason, it is equipped with stiff bristles. Alarmed insects run here and there in the flower, having no idea that they are pollinating it at the same time. When their work is done, the kind *hydnora africana* opens the cage and bids the beetle goodbye. And there it keeps stinking cheerily, waiting for its next suitor.

STINKING CORPSE LILY

Have you ever seen a truly giant plant? Not yet? Well then come closer. Quickly! You won't believe your eyes. What a flower! Meet my pride, *rafflesia arnoldii*. I am so proud of it that I am going to forgive its unfair growing method. This parasitic flower drains the water and nutrients away from woody climbing plants called lianas. This is why it needs neither its own stem nor its own leaves. It just keeps blooming with its huge flower, stinking like forgotten meat at the back of your fridge. If it's lucky, its beautiful red flower with white patches reaches a size of three feet and a respectable weight of 20 pounds. My dear children, you are truly lucky today that you can enjoy its charm because the rare rafflesia unfortunately blooms for only one week before dying off.

QUITE THE ICKY GIANT

TITAN ARUM

It takes time for this darling of mine, native to tropical Asian forests, to bloom. Possibly several years! So be patient. When it finally blooms, though, you will remember it for just as long. Because it stinks to high heaven. Even the less sensitive noses can find its scent within a radius of nearly half a mile. And as it smells like a pile of rotten seafood, flies, which compete for the honor to pollinate it, love it. It is a true race against time, as this dark-violet flower, aptly called "cadaverous," sees this world for a mere three days. When the blooming ends, this proud tropical beauty waits ages to bloom again.

WESTERN SKUNK CABBAGE

Do you want to know how badly a skunk stinks when it feels threatened? Check out the Western skunk cabbage and you'll know right away. Ugh. Not a pleasant scent, I must say, although it comes as no surprise that this stinker prefers growing in mud and in ugly reeking swamps. On the other hand, if you hold your breath for a moment and take a good look at this plant, you may even forgive it for its odor. Is it not beautiful? And it's so hardy, frost is no bother to it, which is why it thrives in North America, even up in Alaska. Furthermore, while its smell makes us a little sick to the stomach, bears waking from hibernation hurry to places where the skunk cabbage grows. They pick and eat it. The reason is because Western skunk cabbage has laxative effects, and after their lengthy sleep throughout the wintertime, bears need to, ahem, you know, empty their bowels.

9

CHAPTER II.

Proceeding onward with our tour, let's go to another area of my incredible botanical garden. Do not hustle, do not shout, and definitely do not trample the plants. And leave your fears at the gate, as this time you will stare in amazement at the peculiar shapes these plants can take. They may look like various objects present in your everyday life. What do you think, kids? If you thought botany was just some boring old hobby for aging gardeners and zealous botanists like myself, I'm sure the next tour will have you running to the nearest florist to buy some seeds, seedlings, pots, and soil in bulk. See for yourselves! For sure there is no one who wouldn't wish to grow a little cup, umbrella, or whatever else. Come in, please, boys and girls! Enter the realm of plants indistinguishable from objects you know very well.

SILVER ARUM

*I*s that a flower or a vase? you ask. Well, your question is very relevant. The bromeliad called *aechmea fasciata*, native to the jungles of South America, is actually also called a vase. The silver vase. And do you happen to know why? Well, take a look at its leathery leaves. What color are they? Green? No way. They're the color of precious metal. And what about the vase? The center of its leaves, arranged in a circular fashion, works as a cup where water can collect and be stored. Of course, water in this silver vase should be replenished regularly. *Aechmea fasciata* is actually very demanding about humidity. It needs water to live, so I visit it every day to moisten it. It rewards me for my care with a beautiful pink flower, which it can proudly bear for up to half a year long.

FLASK-SHAPED PITCHER PLANT

What I am most proud of is my collection of little green flasks. Laughing, are you? Clearly these are not real flasks of glass or wood. These cute containers are just another plant. Stunning, isn't it? To be botanically accurate, these flasks are sophisticated hollow traps, or tubes, which serve to catch their prey. And you heard me correctly—it is prey! The flask-shaped pitcher plant, or *nepenthes ampullaria*, which grows on Indonesian islands, used to be a much-feared carnivorous plant. As time went on, it switched to vegetarian food. Instead of insects, it now catches falling leaves in its flask. The leaf sticks to the open cap, where it goes right into the flask, the plant's belly, where the plant uses a special digestion fluid to transform the leaf to much-needed nutrients. And this happens over and over again.

13

PSYCHOTRIAELATA

Such lips are very kiss-worthy. Flies, bees, bumblebees, and butterflies know this all too well. Bewitched, they keep wandering around the mouth of this beauty. But, my dear flower enthusiasts, the red lips of psychotriaelata are just two attractive leaves hiding a gentle white flower in the middle. This is also why this seemingly seductive but in fact completely innocent plant is sometimes called the bride's lips. If someone in Mexico, where this bigmouthed plant also grows, gives you this flower, it means that he or she likes you. Its red mouths are never truly the same as each other. Similar to human lips, they vary widely in appearance, and the attractive red leaves are all folded into the shape of a different mouth. Are you interested in the lip plant? Would you like to get to know it better? Then you have to go to Central and South America, where it thrives the best.

GLOWING LIPS

LIVING STONE

Blooming stones? Has anyone ever heard of such things, let alone seen them? You must be surprised, shaking your heads in disbelief at all these peculiar scattered pebbles on the ground. "Do they come from the sea?" you ask. No. Absolutely not. These are no stones but flowers. Low succulents that look like stones. And they are actually called "living stones". Please don't kick them anymore! These peculiar flowers are native to dry regions of South Africa, so they are truly modest when it comes to water. When there happens to be enough water, they collect it and store it and keep living and growing happily. Slowly but surely. If the lithops—as this plant is called—opts for it, it can retreat into soil and blend perfectly with its surface. Once in a while these peculiar pebbles get stripped of their old leaves and form new ones. As for blooming, when they blossom a couple of years later, you can enjoy their beauty in bulk. They keep blooming from spring to autumn. I won't hear a bad word about these living stones!

FLAME LILY

Fire, fire! Get the hoses and put out this fire. Ha! Did I fool you? Come on, I would never let fire spread in my botanical garden. I guard it jealously, keeping it safe from everything. This bright flame that is on fire here is in fact the national flower of the African country of Zimbabwe: the well-known flame lily. And it is actually not on fire. You do not have to analyze it long to see that its blossom looks like flames. And like small fires, it flashes over to the neighboring plants, spreading cheerfully.

It can do so thanks to entwining stems at the tips of its leaves. When everything goes well, the lily can reach a respectable height of 10 feet, and it does not mind sandy environments. But be careful and don't burn yourselves. It is just like touching real flames. Adorable as this plant is, there is not a single part of it that is not poisonous. So, definitely do not eat or taste it, and avoid touching it, as it may cause skin problems. There's a reason it looks like real fire.

17

CHAPTER

III.

Whoever has salami, ham, or sausage, eat it fast, as the next part of my botanical garden may prove disastrous for your snacks. You can lose them in the blink of an eye. We are entering the department of true predators among plants, the department of plants ravenous for real meat! I can see some kids are getting startled, stepping back a bit, and other faces look somewhat pale too. What's going on? Are you afraid you'll end up in the belly of a plant? Or get bitten by grassy teeth? Well, don't worry. Do not fear these fragile, carnivorous plants! I am convinced that by the end of our tour you will love them just as I do, which is a lot. Come closer, take a look!

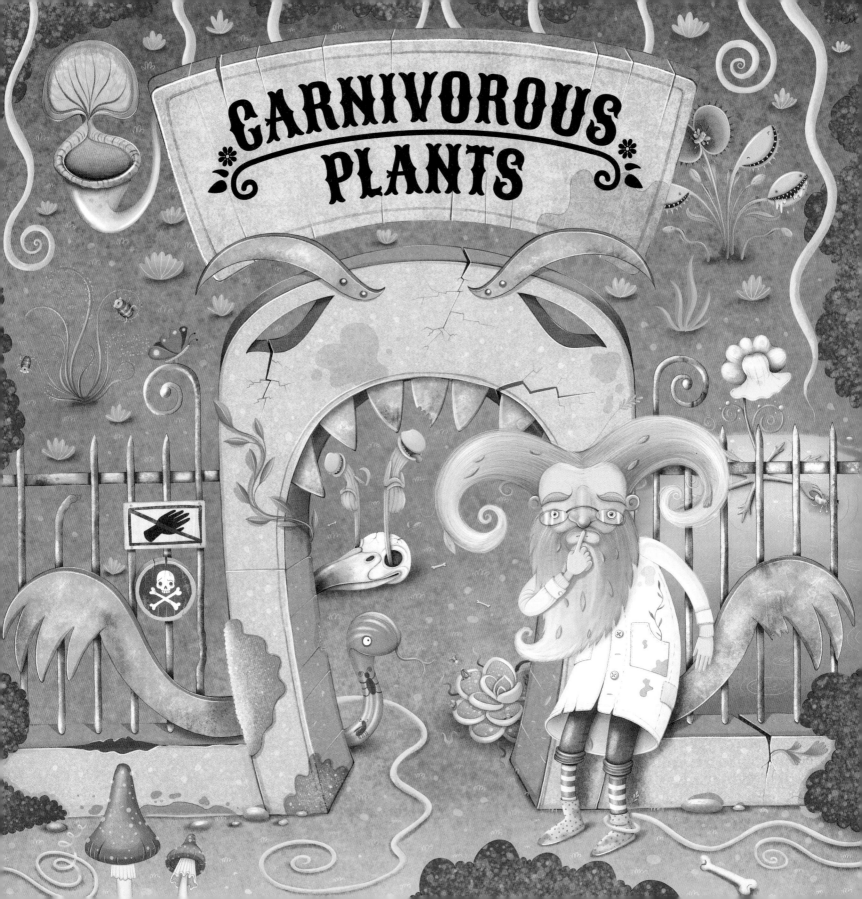

CARNIVOROUS PLANTS

VENUS FLYTRAP

Shhh! Silence, children. Unfortunate creatures are approaching a Venus flytrap, an eager hunter of all spiders, flies, and ants. Take a look. They have already noticed the plant. The flytrap attracts insects with its color and sweet nectar produced by glands on leaves. But the leaves form a trap. The insect is running towards the plant, touching the plant's hairs with its long legs. The flytrap is biding its time. It is going to snap shut only when the touch is repeated multiple times within a short period. This is the plant's protection from false alarms. Because each empty shutting is exhausting and damages the plant. And there it is! The trap has closed and the prey stands no chance. The plant will be digesting it for a week. Then there will be time for another hunt.

CALIFORNIA PITCHER PLANT

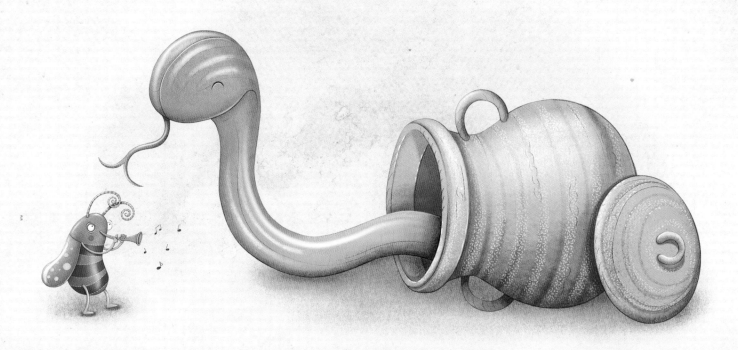

At first sight it might seem like you're watching the raised head of a lurking cobra, but don't worry! This is not a snake. They just look similar. We remain in the realm of plants, and you, my dear children, are just watching another carnivorous plant of mine: the California pitcher plant, or darlingtonia. This flower's leaves have practically turned into tubes that are insect traps. Some are up to 35 inches tall, while others are smaller and rest on the ground. The smart cobra lily can catch truly diverse prey. The light tube head (the one resembling a snake's head) attracts insects with its color and with the sweet nectar it produces. Beetles drop their guard. Thinking they are entering an innocent flower, they descend deeper and deeper into the tube. When they realize their fatal mistake, it is too late. It's impossible to get back up.

CAPE SUNDEW

My young friends, take note of the tiny droplets shining on the hairs covering its leaves. This is the ingenious trap of another carnivorous plant—the Cape sundew. Sweet-toothed insects come to its leaves to savor its sweet juice, but as soon as this happens, leaves start winding around their little bodies, coiling them around just like octopus tentacles. No matter how much the fly or ant might try, there is no escape from this trap. When all leaves wind around the prey, the sundew forms a sort of outer stomach and starts digesting its victim. No one would guess that the innocent-looking pink flowering plant is such a ruthless predator. But, well, every being in nature is striving for survival.

RAJAH
PITCHER PLANT

Anyone carrying his favorite pet may lose it if he gets too close to the raja pitcher plant, the biggest carnivorous plant. Yes, my dear friends, that's it over there. This almost 20-foot-tall flower from Borneo wouldn't say no to a small mammal for lunch. It needs something to live on. Take a close look. Isn't it fascinating? When it swallows its prey, it closes the cap, so that its feast—or rather, the digestion process—is not disrupted by rain. It opens to the world right when it gets hungry again. No one is safe from it, except for the mountain treeshrew. This tiny rodent befriended the pitcher plant. It enters its vial cheerfully, drinks its sweet nectar, and then defecates in its tube. The pitcher plant does not mind, as the droppings are a source of beneficial nitrogen. This is why it never eats a treeshrew, no matter how hungry it is.

TRUMPET
PITCHER

Originating in North America, elegant trumpet pitchers use the same hunting tactics as other carnivorous plants. They lure their prey with their attractive appearance and tasty nectar. In a jiffy, they then shift the caught insects into their long tubes. This is called a gravity trap. Everything falls down and no one manages to get back up. Trumpet pitchers are quite active hunters. Sometimes they catch more prey than they can devour.

The victim's bodies then decompose in the pitcher's tube, which is not good for the plant. If you choose to grow trumpet pitchers at home, plug their traps from time to time and let them relax from hunting for a while. In North America, they grow in swamps by the Atlantic, which means they need a lot of water and light to thrive.

MEXICAN BUTTERWORT

Let's watch the butterwort, its rich leaves covered in little beetles. They have been literally glued to the leaves. The butterwort covers its leaves with a slimy, sticky, and glittering substance that lures beetles and then does not let them get away. They remain on the leaves and then the butterwort gradually and quietly digests them. Interestingly, butterworts only hunt in summer in the dry period, and in winter they shift to vegetarian food. During that time, they focus on retaining as much water in their leaves as possible. If you wish to take a trip to see Mexican butterworts, go to the mountainous regions of Mexico and Central America, where they thrive on limestone rocks.

26

BLADDERWORT

Don't worry. The next flower is not going to trap you in its net. It loves meat, that is true, but not human meat. It eats water worms, water fleas, and insect larvae, so there is no need to get upset. Carnivorous bladderworts grow in lakes, streams, and flooded and waterlogged soil. Do not search for roots. There is just a stem and leaves. They drift freely over the water's surface, literally drawing their helpless victims into their side bladders. A mere half-hour from a successful hunting attempt, the bladderworts are ready for action again. They are simply insatiable. However, not all bladderworts can be found in water. As they rank among the most common species of carnivorous plants, some are adapted to terrestrial life. However, they have one thing in common: their beautiful flowers.

CHAPTER

IV.

My dear curious children. Honestly, do you wish to continue? Forcing our way through the bushes of my botanical garden, discovering unique plants, and wondering about the incredible beauty and resourcefulness of plants and their blossoms? You are nodding yes, so let's keep moving forward. Next, I would like to show you plants that will first make you think they are not flowers but rather something else. Or even *someone* else! Someone different. Like an animal or a person. Whoever doubts, come and look, and don't protest that I'm pulling your leg! I am going to show you absolute rarities that no other collector in the world has and, in fact, cannot have. Yes, because I am the only one! I live with plants and I may even be turning into a plant! I do not tame them. I let them live freely. I let them grow and spread. So, let's not waste time with idle talk. Let's discover these next flowers, gentle creatures that look like a naked guy or a duck.

PARROT FLOWER

Keep your eyes wide open and hold your breath. I am proud to present the most precious piece of the whole of my improbable plant collection. Abrakadabra! Feast your eyes. Rejoice in this enormous beauty. These plants bear the Latin name *impatiens psittacina* and they bloom with little parrots. Really. If you don't believe me, check for yourselves up close. Take a look, as they are cheerily flying on their stems, violet with crimson heads like they're real! My dear children, what I am presenting now is truly unique. This plant grows in the wild in a small area of Northern Thailand. And its export is strictly forbidden! So very few people may see it with their own eyes. This is something you should prize. So take a while to enjoy the presence of a one-and-a-half-foot tall, richly branching, and flowering parrot flower.

LARGE DUCK ORCHID

Let's stay with plants resembling feathered animals for a while. My dear friends of plant life, aren't these Australian orchids—the blossoms of which look like they are going to quack like a duck—magnificent? Their colorful blossoms use their intoxicating scent to lure insects for pollination from spring to summer. As soon as the crazy males get close to this dazzling orchid and land in the beak of its blossom, they are literally trapped. Before they can get out, though, they are all covered in life-giving pollen. Just like parrot flowers, large duck orchids grow only in the Australian wilderness, as their existence depends on the presence of a special Australian fungus growing in local eucalyptus forests.

SWADDLED BABIES

HALF HUMAN HALF PLANT

Please be quiet. Don't wake my babies. I have lots of them here and it would be true turmoil if they all started crying. We would have to plug our ears or hush the little ones, and that is not an easy task. Ha, ha! I got you! Don't worry about my babies. They are silent and do not cry. Actually, they're not babies at all. Meet the *anguloa uniflora*, an orchid, at home in the mountains of the Peruvian Andes. The gentle babies are wrapped in a diaper, as you might already see, using the snow-white flowers of this orchid. Their flowers attract insects closer. Beetles are lured and *wham!* They are taken by surprise, shaking in the babies' bellies, bathing in their pollen. Luckily, they always find a way out—to spread *anguloa uniflora* further and further over the Andes.

33

BEE ORCHID

Buzz, buzz, buzz. Can you hear it? Those bees buzzing all around? Ha! I fooled you yet again, my dear children. There's nothing buzzing around. Watch carefully the pinkish blossoms of the bee orchid. The bodies of bees seemingly sitting on it are just a decoy. They are a part of the flower that merely poses as insect females. And why is that? They use this marvelous similarity to lure males, who lovingly gravitate toward them without noticing they're pollinating the bee orchid. Yes, yes, you heard me correctly. Flowers and plants can be quite cunning. And the bee orchid is autogamous, meaning if there are not enough insects, it can pollinate itself. It needs lots of sun to live, so it proudly and abundantly rises in meadows in the Mediterranean.

DANCING GIRL IMPATIENS

Let's proceed further, deeper and deeper into my botanical garden, where everything is growing, thriving, curling, and crawling. Tell me, my dear ones, who among you would like to dance? All of you? Great! Let's turn the music on and start dancing, whirling with the beautiful African impatiens—called *impatiens bequaertii* in Latin—a rare plant that blooms with tiny white or light-pink dancers, fragile little girls in fluffy skirts with wide-open arms. These beautiful ballerinas, at home in the tropical forests of East Africa, have one incredible gift: they can take root anywhere they touch the ground. They then grow and blossom, and their flowers whirl in rhythm with the breeze, while their dark-green, heart-shaped leaves clap along with those little dancers.

NAKED MAN ORCHID

And now, dear girls and boys, meet one of the most common orchids in the Mediterranean. You can find it growing thickly along the coast, next to roads, and on bushy ground. Don't turn your noses up and don't turn away saying you're uninterested in such an ordinary and commonplace plant. Take a closer look! Don't their light-to dark-pink flowers remind you of figurines? Naked man orchids start blooming in April and keep blooming throughout May. Luckily, they are unashamed of their nakedness. Quite the opposite. Like I said, most of them are pink, but on rare occasions they can be white.

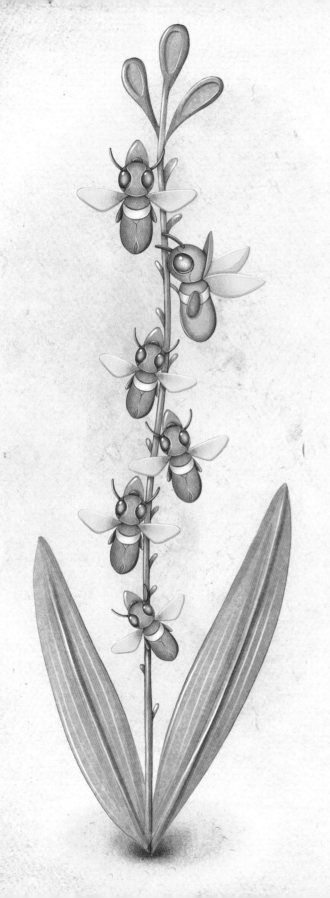

FLY ORCHID

Everyone who wishes to look deeper into my paradise of flowers, plants, and herbs is now getting a fly swatter. When the fly orchid is present, you'll need it. Oh, no! What are you doing? Please, do not hit the *plant* with the fly swatter! It seems that it is covered in flies from top to bottom, but in this case, these are not flies. If you've been paying attention during our tour of this part of my garden, it's surely apparent that these are blossoms. Insects are just bound to arrive. Insect males smell the pheromone scent produced by its flowers, and it drives them crazy. As you now know, my dear children, flowers will do whatever it takes to survive. These are the ways of nature. One cannot be surprised that they grow abundantly throughout Europe.

CHAPTER
V.

Do you like trees? If so, it's time to enter another section of my botanical garden. The part filled with giants with trunks, branches, and crowns. Trees can be very different, my dear young visitors. There are trees that strangle. Others are rainbow colored, others have prickles over their bodies like prehistoric dinosaurs, and still others bloom at night. Some trees are ancient, others are sacred. Some are small, others almost rise to the sky. And they all have one thing in common. They all are beautiful, stunning, and charming. Oh, how I admire them, feeling so good in their presence. Breathe in, breath out. Spread your arms out and absorb the energy from my unique tree collection.

JAVA COTTON

Take a look at the towering Java cotton tree, a titan native to Latin American forests. I's clear why this tree that's 12 stories tall has been held sacred by the local indigenous Amazonian tribes and why they associate it with forest spirits. If you come across a *ceiba pentandra*—as it's known in Latin—at night, you may be puzzled by the unusual cheesy smell produced by its flowers, which open at sunset to attract bats. Yes, that is correct. Bats! Who else but those flying mammals could pollinate such a giant? When the *ceiba* is young, its trunk is covered in dangerous-looking prickles. As time passes, they fall off and the supporting roots gain enough strength to keep this giant upright, even when the inside of its trunk molders away. Indeed, the *ceiba* deserves some respect!

GRAPETREE

Oh my, I can see that you are taken by surprise by yet another botanical curiosity of mine: the Brazilian grapetree. No worries. Pick as much fruit as you wish. They are healthy and filled with vitamin C. You may be surprised to see them grow right from the stems or old branches. Just as its creamy-white flowers do. As the tree blooms up to six times a year, there's always something nice to watch. In its home country, the Brazilian grapetree—also called jabuticaba—reaches a height of 50 feet, so it is no pipsqueak, truly. But if you opt for planting a grapetree at home, be ready for its very, very slow growth. It can take decades before it reaches the height of an average apple tree. Yes, yes, patience and care are essential. As it is genetically bound to love warmth, this tree may be hurt by medium frost.

RAINBOW EUCALYPTUS

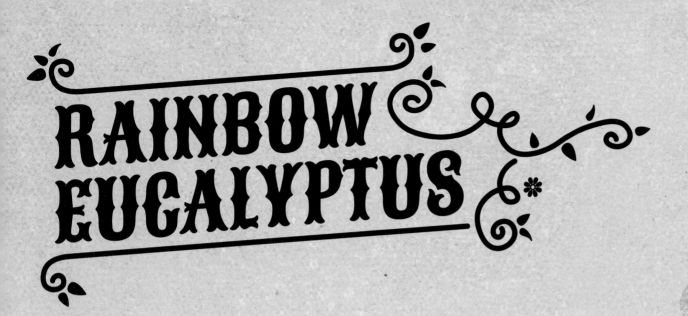

My dear young friends, please don't distrust me. I have not used any acrylics or watercolors to secretly paint rainbow stripes on this tree's trunk. No, no, I really have nothing to do with it. It's all natural. Native to the Philippines, the rainbow eucalyptus is truly rainbow-colored from birth. The colored bands are actually stripes that are bared when the eucalyptus's overlying bark naturally peels off. Well, this peculiar skin sloughing makes a remarkable sight. These unique eucalyptus trees grow like weeds. Really. They can grow a full 30 feet in just over a year. Another advantage is that they perfectly strengthen soil damaged by erosion. Oh great, you might be saying. Unfortunately, these colorful beauties need warmth. Where there is cold, they simply do not thrive.

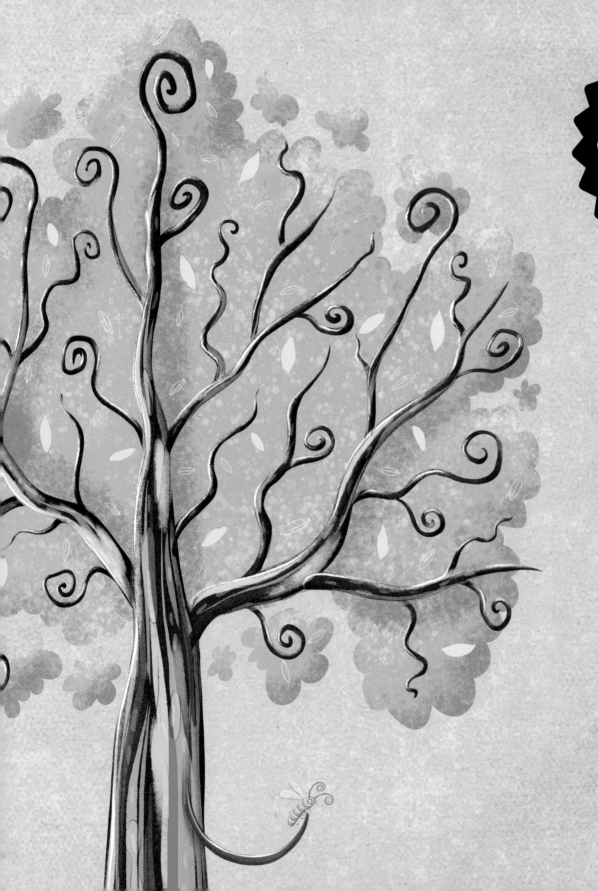

TREE FROM
A DREAM

STRANGLER FIG

I am launching a search for the most famous strangler in the world—the strangler fig. To survive and grow, these figs first have to strangle their host tree. How does this happen? A bird or another animal leaves a seed in some crack in a tree. The seed sprouts and starts growing root runners. They then wrap around the host's trunk and climb up toward the sun. As it grows and gains strength, its roots gain strength too, tightening their loop more and more firmly. Over time, the host dies. A life for a life. On the other hand, as they grow, these figs protect their host trees from tropical cyclones. And hollows formed by the strangler fig's roots offer shelter to many tropical animals.

DRAGON'S BLOOD TREE

If you wish to see this dragon tree with your own eyes, head for the island of Socotra in the Arabian Sea. That's where this charming tree with an umbrella-like treetop grows. The majestic shape of its crown is not random. It provides cooling shade to protect its small seedlings from the hot sun, which would otherwise destroy them before they gain strength and grow up. It also reduces water evaporation. If you cut into this tree, red blood will run from it. The liquid isn't really blood, though. It's resin and sap that's merely the *color* of blood. To this very day, this tree's so-called dragon blood is used to varnish violins.

CHAPTER

VI.

Our next tour, my friends, will be of a special corner of my unique botanical garden. More specifically, I will be taking you to the realm of mushrooms and fungi—plants that belong to the most ancient organisms on our blue planet. After all, they already grew here in the ancient Proterozoic eon, which, if my calculations are correct, started over a billion years ago. Well, that is something! And you'll be amazed even more when I say that at present there are over 8.7 million fungal species living on Earth. Incredible! You won't believe what these beings can do. They can control and tame ants and shed blood, tears, and azure milk. And they stink to high heaven and look like aliens. So, my dear little friends, without any further ado, let's start our fungal adventure.

INDIGO
MILK CAP

You definitely know boletes, champignons, or amanitas, but I am convinced that you have never seen what I am now about to show you in the fungi corner of my botanical garden. A perfectly blue mushroom. It is called the indigo milk cap, and it grows in the deciduous and coniferous forests of North and Central America and East Asia. Most of all, it thrives in rain and in the presence of pine trees. My dear ones, I assure you, in the whole world there is no other mushroom so perfectly blue. The younger it is, the deeper the blue. It gets lighter with age. When this beauty with a lightly earthy smell is cut, it sheds indigo blue milk, which turns green over time due to air exposure. Nothing lasts forever, my friends, not even this gorgeous azure color. In addition to its extravagantly colored charms, this mushroom is also edible. It tastes sugary and is best grilled!

ANEMONE STINKHORN

What's that smell? I see you are searching for the source of this horrible odor. Well, keep searching, but let me give you one piece of advice. Look a bit lower. Even lower. Down to the ground. Bingo, you've caught the strange stinker by the tail. By its tentacle, actually. No, it is no alien or sea anemone that mistook the wood for the ocean, although at first sight it might seem so. But back to reality. Here before us is an Australian fungus called *aseroe rubra*. It is no surprise for Australians, as it is very common there.

What smells like rotten meat on the fungus is the dark-brown slime it excretes. Please excuse the unpleasantness. Like flowers, *aseroe rubra* needs to attract insects to successfully spread its spores around. When its life begins, *aseroe* looks like a small egg buried in the ground. Later on, it develops its strange beauty. And if its insect hunt is successful, *aseroe* spreads tremendously fast. Ages ago, you would have only found it in Australia, but by now it is at home in New Zealand and has spread throughout the entire world.

BLEEDING TOOTH FUNGUS

Let me introduce you to the bleeding tooth fungus. The red liquid flowing out of the delicate pores of this fungus prove that it is a young mushroom. Lean a bit closer to its cap. Can you see it? It is covered with fine hair. This hair is going to fall out over time and the whole cap will turn gray, brown, and stiff, and the splendor will be gone. The beautiful bleeding tooth fungus grows nearly throughout the entire world. It needs certain species of spruce and fir trees, with whom it lives in perfect symbiosis. This mushroom helps its host trees absorb minerals important for their growth. In exchange, the trees offer the mushroom invaluable carbon. Also, the blood coming from the fungi is used as an environmentally friendly dye for textiles.

ROTTEN OR BEAUTIFUL?

VIOLET CORAL

There is no need to fetch a diving mask, although it looks like we're on the seabed. This peculiar mushroom of Irish origin, *clavaria zollingeri*, which looks exactly like some sea corals, is commonly called the violet coral. Up to four inches high, with a thick stem dividing into numerous branches and forks, it has a beautiful violet color. Nature can play wonderful games. As these mushrooms, which grow in grass and

moss, get old, their beautiful color starts fading and they turn gray. Their beauty sometimes sustains the same damage after heavy rains. Scientists have discovered—and I, as an avid botanist, can confirm—that these mushrooms help significantly with the decomposition of dead grass as well as moss. And that's the way it's supposed to be. Everything in the world has its important and unmistakable role.

ZOMBIE MUSHROOM

The quiet part of our tour gets us swiftly but elegantly to a somewhat scary part of my fungi corner. I am going to show you a genuine zombie fungus. It is a Brazilian mushroom called *ophiocordyceps unilateralis*, the spores of which infiltrate the bodies of ants and then start controlling their behavior. The poor creature may wish to stay in its anthill but is forced to leave, find a leaf, bite into it, and hold it until it runs out of power and dies. This is precisely the moment the *ophiocordyceps unilateralis* is waiting for. It instantly fills the tiny black body with further spores, later shooting them into the nearby anthill. Yes, sweethearts, these spores infect more ant workers. And while those hard-working insects die, the zombie fungi multiply cheerfully.

CORDYCEPS

The Brazilian ophiocordyceps is not the only zombie mushroom. There is another fungal monster I would like to show you. It is called caterpillar fungus. In springtime, it hatches out of the mycelium—the vegetative part of a fungus—like any other peaceful mushroom, but listen carefully. Soon after its struggle for survival begins, it turns into a bloodthirsty beast. It shoots its spores onto insect and starts multiplying in their bodies.

Before the unfortunate victim dies, it starts forming the most bizarre fungal offshoots! Some caterpillar fungi attack caterpillars preparing to spend winter underground. Having the fungal spores in their tummies, they nicely bury themselves in the ground and then are literally devoured by the predatory fungus. When springtime comes, there will be no caterpillar rising to the surface but the caterpillar mushroom.

PANELLUS STIPTICUS

Are you wondering why I'm about to show you a totally common mushroom called the bitter oyster? A mushroom with no remarkable or surprising appearance? With neither a pleasant nor an unpleasant smell? Is there anything interesting at all about this fungus, which grows from fallen branches or moldered stumps of all sorts? Just a moment. I am going to switch the light off and you are going to see for yourselves. The bitter oyster glows gently around the world just like a lost marsh fairy. Doesn't it feel like a fairy tale? It can glow like fireflies, using the same principle, called bioluminescence. You are aware that a shining bulb is hot. But if you come across a glowing bitter oyster, it will not burn you. Its light is cold. I am going to tell you about the great mystery of the bitter oyster, which I am trying to unravel. Bitter oysters in Europe do not glow, but in America they glow far and wide.

CHAPTER

VII.

My dearest botany enthusiasts, we are approaching the very end of our expedition. It's the last pavilion, which should be fenced off and guarded 24/7. Because anyone unfortunate enough to stray over here would go mad with fear. This is why I save it for the end of our tour. Because this section hides plants that are dreadful, horrifying, thorny, and big-eyed. If you, my friends, can cope with this part of the tour, you can deem yourselves experts in extreme botany, just like me. Maybe I will take you in for an internship—unpaid of course. A fellow who is not scared easily always comes in handy. Now then, hold on tight. The gates to the eerie pavilion are opening!

WHITE BANEBERRY

I can see you trembling with fear, afraid to enter the shadowy spot of my garden from where the eyes of white baneberry, the plant that earned the horrible nickname "doll's-eyes," are watching you! Actually, these are white fruits with black spots in the middle. They grow plentifully on red stems, haunting everyone with their googly eyes. They give you a fright but they wouldn't hurt you. Of course, do not try to gobble them up, as they are highly poisonous. The white baneberry, at three feet tall, grows in the broad-leaved forests of North America. In May, its notched leaves are enriched with little fragrant, alabaster blossoms, which at the end of July turn into haunting eyes.

BLACK BAT

Take a good look here, children. Those of you who are afraid of bats should walk a few steps away, as you may not feel too well close to this plant! Its pitch-black blossom looks strikingly like a bat. More specifically, like a bat endowed with long whiskers. An interesting combination, and a spooky one, one might even say a Halloween-like combination. As this black bat-like flower blooms at the end of summertime, everything suggests that it desires to be perfectly ready for the October festival of the dead. If you're growing fond of this dark Asian beauty, collect its seeds in your pockets and plant them at home. If you offer it some tropical moisture, tropical heat, and a spacious pot where it can comfortably stretch its roots, it will repay you for your efforts. It looks like a sneering bat but it is grateful, believe me!

CRISTATA

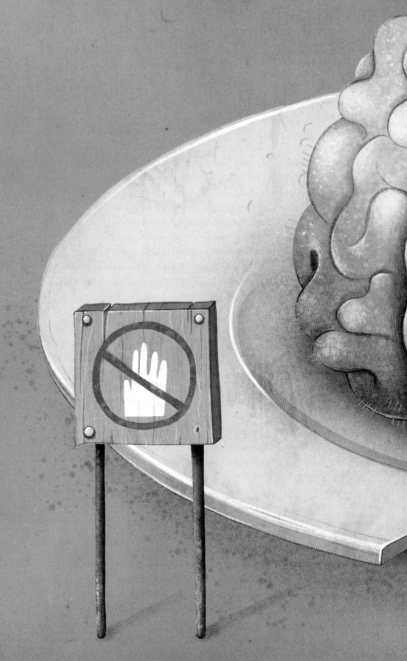

I am growing a spare brain for myself. When the one in my head becomes erratic, the new one will come in handy. Hahaha, don't make such terrified faces! It's just my attempt at dark humor. I would hardly stuff a cactus into my head, even though it resembles a human brain with absolute perfection. I know, I know. It is not gray-white like a real brain—it is bright green. At any rate, this cactus brain is formed by a cluster of curved stems that somehow twist around and around each other. Unlike a true brain, which blooms solely with interesting ideas, this little plant brain is decorated with real flowers, which bloom in the springtime. And which country may pride itself on being home to cactus brains? Why, Mexico in Central America.

THE BRAIN
CACTUS

DEVIL'S HAND

Proceed carefully and stay quiet as a mouse. Because we are approaching a tree from which the devil's hands bloom. Yellow and red palms with five fingers. Be extra careful. Do not fall into their clutches. But no, no, do not cry, let's calm you down. *Chiranthodendron pentadactylon* won't harm any of you. On the contrary! Its horrible-looking blossoms are an important component of medicines for heart problems, so calm down, slow down your breathing, and calm the beating of your alarmed hearts. The devil's hand grows in Mexican forests and long ago it used to belong among trees particularly revered by the Aztecs. Though the devil's hand prefers warm tropical climates, it grows in colder conditions as well because it is extremely hardy.

PORCUPINE
TOMATO

Is there anyone who has not been scared a little bit, yet? Whose voice did not tremble a bit? Who dares continue our tour? Everyone's volunteering? You are remarkably courageous, I must admit. However, I dare say that in the presence of this little flower, you need to stay on guard. The blue-green leaves of this tropical perm are covered with sharp orange thorns! And not only its leaves are armed to the teeth.

Even the fruit of this Madagascar plant, which is related to tomatoes, are armed. However, while the devil's thorn might break your teeth, that wouldn't be the worst part, as the whole of the plant, from tips to toes, is poisonous. Its gentle violet blossoms with yellow centers look innocent and attract beetles, bees, and bumblebees, but squirrels and other small rodents avoid this devilish flower from afar.

INDEX

www.albatrosbooks.com

© Designed by B4U Publishing for Albatros, an imprint of Albatros Media Group, 2022. 5. května 22, Prague 4, Czech Republic.
Author: Štěpánka Sekaninová, Illustrator: Zuzana Dreadka Krutá

ISBN: 978-80-00-06353-9